Paw Prints

Rottweilers

by Nadia Higgins

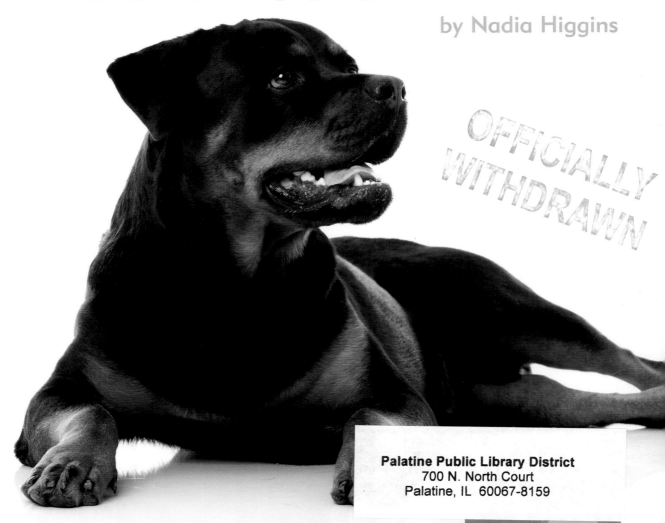

Ideas for Parents and Teachers

Bullfrog Books let children practice reading informational text at the earliest reading levels. Repetition, familiar words, and photo labels support early readers.

Before Reading

- Discuss the cover photo. What does it tell them?

- Look at the picture glossary together. Read and discuss the words.

Read the Book

- "Walk" through the book and look at the photos. Let the child ask questions. Point out the photo labels.

- Read the book to the child, or have him or her read independently.

After Reading

- Prompt the child to think more. Ask: Have you ever seen a Rottweiler? Were you surprised by how big it was?

Bullfrog Books are published by Jump!
5357 Penn Avenue South
Minneapolis, MN 55419
www.jumplibrary.com

Library of Congress Cataloging-in-Publication Data

Names: Higgins, Nadia, author.
Title: Rottweilers / by Nadia Higgins.
Description: Minneapolis, MN : Jump!, Inc., 2018.
Series: Paw prints
Series: Bullfrog books | Includes index.
Audience: Ages 5 to 8. | Audience: Grades K to 3.
Identifiers: LCCN 2017044076 (print)
LCCN 2017044360 (ebook)
ISBN 9781624967856 (ebook)
ISBN 9781624967849 (hardcover : alk. paper)
Subjects: LCSH: Rottweiler dog—Juvenile literature.
Classification: LCC SF429.R7 (ebook)
LCC SF429.R7 H54 2018 (print) | DDC 636.73—dc23
LC record available at https://lccn.loc.gov/2017044076

Editor: Jenna Trnka
Book Designer: Molly Ballanger

Photo Credits: GlobalP/iStock, cover; Dora Zett/Shutterstock, 1, 24; Ermolaev Alexander/Shutterstock, 3; Don Hebert/Getty, 4, 23tr; cynoclub/Shutterstock, 5; John Daniels/Pantheon/SuperStock, 6–7; Ammit Jack/Shutterstock, 8, 23tl; Grigorita Ko/Shutterstock, 9, 17, 23bl, 23br; Mark Raycroft/Minden Pictures/SuperStock, 10–11, 23mr; Denis Kuvaev/Shutterstock, 12–13; Tatiana Makotra/Shutterstock, 13, 23ml; Merrimon Crawford/Shutterstock, 14–15; Juniors Bildarchiv/Age Fotostock, 16; gilangtristiano/Shutterstock, 18–19; Tierfotoagentur/Alamy, 20–21; Oktay Ortakcioglu/iStock, 22.

Printed in the United States of America at Corporate Graphics in North Mankato, Minnesota.

Table of Contents

Loyal Rotties

This is a loyal dog.

What kind of dog is it?

A Rottweiler!

Some people say Rottie for short.

5

Rotties protect their families.

These dogs have big heads.

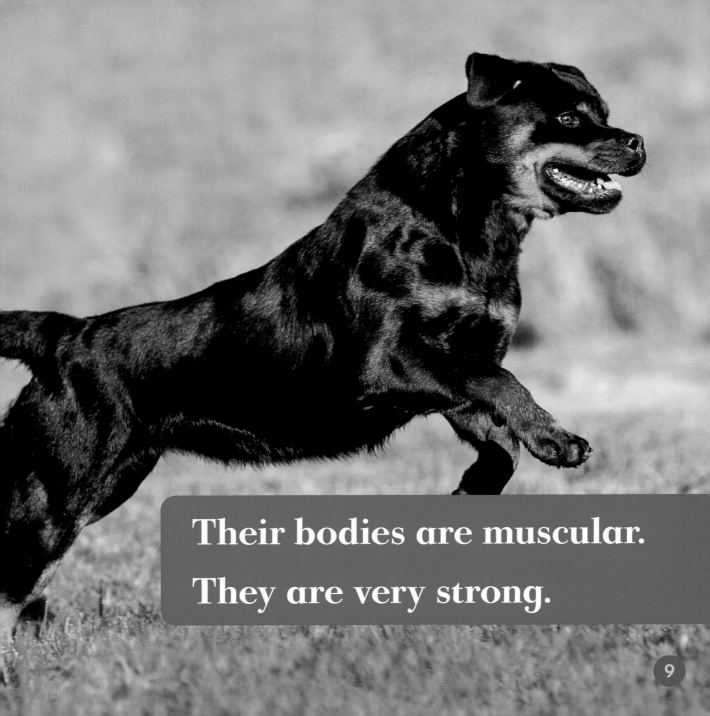

Their bodies are muscular.

They are very strong.

A Rottie is always black.
It has tan markings.
Look at those eyebrows!

eyebrows

Pet it!

Its coat feels coarse.

coat

Rotties learn fast.

They like to run.

They like
to play, too.

This one fetches a ball!

17

Come. Sit. Stay.

Rotties want
to please you.

Good dog!

Rotties are gentle giants.
They will be loyal to you.
Do you want a Rottie?

A Rottweiler Up Close

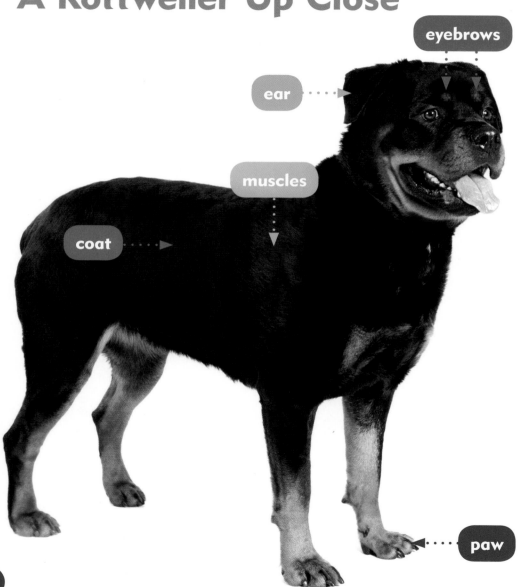

eyebrows

ear

muscles

coat

paw

Picture Glossary

coarse
Thick and wiry.

loyal
Faithful.

coat
A dog's fur.

markings
Marks or patterns
on a dog's coat.

fetches
Goes after
something and
brings it back.

muscular
Having strong
muscles.

Index

To Learn More

Learning more is as easy as 1, 2, 3.

1) Go to www.factsurfer.com

2) Enter "rottweilers" into the search box.

3) Click the "Surf" button to see a list of websites.

With factsurfer.com, finding more information is just a click away.